Be a
Community
Leader

How to
Give a Speech

Leslie Harper

PowerKiDS press™
New York

Published in 2015 by The Rosen Publishing Group, Inc.
29 East 21st Street, New York, NY 10010

First Edition

Editor: Norman Graubart
Book Design: Joe Carney
Book Layout: Colleen Bialecki
Photo Research: Katie Stryker

Photo Credits: Cover Steve Debenport/E+/Getty Images; p. 4 Alexander Novikov/iStock/Thinkstock; p. 5 Gary John Norman/Iconica/Getty Images; p. 6 Rolls Press/Popperphoto/Getty Images; p. 7 Jon Levy/AFP/Getty Images; pp. 9, 13 SW Productions/Stockbyte/Getty Images; p. 10 moodboard/Thinkstock; p. 11 Comstock Images/Stockbyte/Thinkstock; p. 12 pojoslaw/iStock/Thinkstock; p. 15 Creatas Images/Thinkstock; p. 16 Roberaten/Shutterstock.com; p. 17 Jonathan Ross/Hemera/Thinkstock; p. 18 Photos.com/Thinkstock; p. 19 Fuse/Thinkstock; p. 20 Klaus Tiedge/Blend Images/Thinkstock; p. 21 Jupiterimages/BananaStock /Thinkstock; p. 22 Anthony Lee/OJO Images/Getty Images; p. 23 Caiaimage/Martin Barraud/Brand X Pictures/Getty Images; p. 25 Thinkstock Images/Stockbyte/Thinkstock; p. 26 Image Source/Getty Images; p. 27 Yellow Dog Productions/The Image Bank/Getty Images; p. 29 vm/iStock/Thinkstock; p. 30 Thinkstock /Stockbyte/Thinkstock.

Library of Congress Cataloging-in-Publication Data

Harper, Leslie.
 How to give a speech / by Leslie Harper. — First edition.
    pages cm. — (Be a community leader)
 Includes index.
 Includes webliography.
 ISBN 978-1-4777-6697-2 (library binding) — ISBN 978-1-4777-6700-9 (pbk.) —
ISBN 978-1-4777-6698-9 (6-pack)
 1. Public speaking—Juvenile literature. I. Title.
 PN4129.15.H375 2014
 808.5'1—dc23
                        2014004545

Manufactured in the United States of America

CPSIA Compliance Information: Batch #WS14PK3: For Further Information contact Rosen Publishing, New York, New York at 1-800-237-9932

Contents

Speak Up!

Have you ever had to speak in front of your class? Perhaps you were asked how you solved a math problem or what you did over summer vacation. When a person talks to a group of people, it is called giving a speech.

Some speeches are meant to give information about a topic or explain how something works. Others are meant to **persuade**, or convince, people to think a certain way or take a certain action. Activists, or people who take action for what they believe is right, give speeches to persuade people.

> Giving a speech involves several skills. You have to organize ideas, write good notes, and speak well.

Many others, including business leaders, scientists, and lawyers give speeches as part of their jobs. Politicians and other elected officials often give speeches in front of hundreds, or even thousands, of people.

A speech does not have to be in front of a crowd of thousands to be important, though. By using the right words and presenting them in the right way, you can give a speech that may make a real difference in your school or community!

Speech Tips

Effective speeches can be any length, as long as you reach your goal of informing or persuading. In 1863, President Abraham Lincoln gave a speech called the Gettysburg Address, which was only 2 minutes long. Today it is one of the most famous speeches in history.

Famous Speeches

Throughout history, effective speakers have used words to change people's minds. Great speeches can **motivate** people to take action. In 1963, Dr. Martin Luther King Jr. gave his famous "I Have a Dream" speech at a rally in Washington, DC. The speech called for equality for all people and an end to racial discrimination. The next year, the US government passed the Civil Rights Act of 1964. King was awarded the Nobel Peace Prize for his work in the civil rights movement.

Martin Luther King Jr. delivered his "I Have a Dream" speech on August 28, 1963. His words made many Americans change their minds about racism and civil rights.

Nelson Mandela was the first black president of South Africa. Here, he gives a speech at the United Nations.

Other activists have used powerful speeches to change laws, too. Before 1920, many women in the United States did not have suffrage, or the right to vote in elections. American women started the women's suffrage movement to argue for their right to vote. One of their leaders, Susan B. Anthony, traveled the country giving nearly 100 speeches a year. Her speeches encouraged people to support voting rights for women.

An effective speech can also move and inspire people. Leaders such as Franklin Delano Roosevelt, Winston Churchill, and Nelson Mandela have used speeches to bring people together in times of trouble.

Choosing an Issue

When Martin Luther King Jr. gave his "I Have a Dream" speech, he wanted to inspire people to treat each other as equals. What would you like to inspire people to feel or do? When you are thinking of a topic for your speech, think about what is important to you. Do you feel strongly about environmental issues? Do you care about protecting animals? Are you passionate about making your school or neighborhood a better place?

You may find it helpful to read your local newspaper or talk to adults who are active in your community. You may learn about a problem or issue that you would like to help solve. For example, you may learn that some people at your school and in your neighborhood are concerned about bullying. One way to help solve the problem would be to encourage people to talk to adults about bullying incidents. Another could be to start an antibullying club.

Bullying is a problem that affects both kids and adults. It would be a great speech topic.

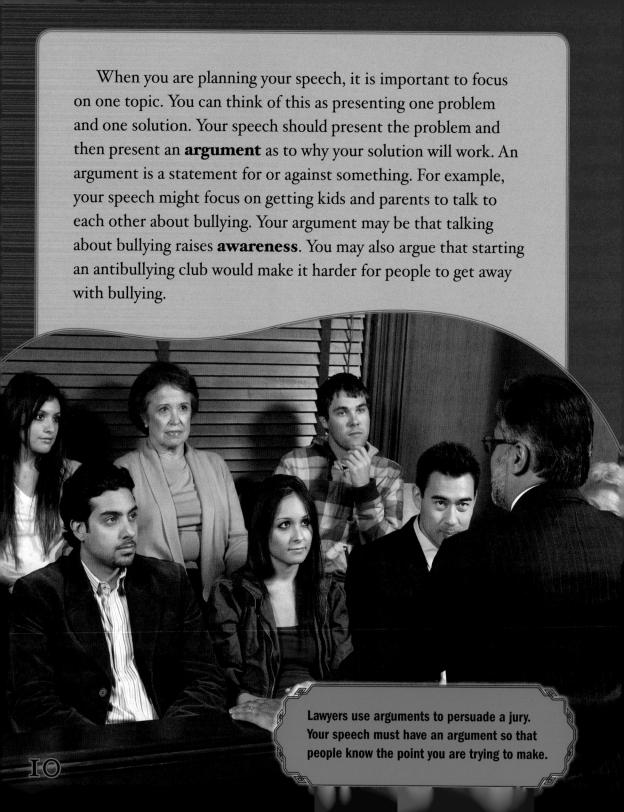

When you are planning your speech, it is important to focus on one topic. You can think of this as presenting one problem and one solution. Your speech should present the problem and then present an **argument** as to why your solution will work. An argument is a statement for or against something. For example, your speech might focus on getting kids and parents to talk to each other about bullying. Your argument may be that talking about bullying raises **awareness**. You may also argue that starting an antibullying club would make it harder for people to get away with bullying.

Lawyers use arguments to persuade a jury. Your speech must have an argument so that people know the point you are trying to make.

You may care about a lot of different issues.
Still, you must focus your speech on one issue.
This is called clarity.

You may also have other ideas as to how to improve your community. You may think there should be more traffic lights on the roads and that your local park should get new grass. However, those are topics for different speeches. By keeping your speech focused on one issue, it will be less likely that listeners will get confused about your argument.

Pick a Place

The place where you choose to give your speech is important. To help you decide on a location, you should first figure out who your **audience** will be. Your audience is the group of people who will listen to you. If your topic relates to your school, for example, your audience may be your classmates. It could also be teachers or members of your local school board. If you want your local government to take action or change a law, you may want to speak at a city council meeting where elected officials can listen.

You may get a chance to speak at a city council meeting. If so, your audience will be both the city council and the other people attending the meeting.

If your topic relates to your entire community, as the bullying topic does, then your audience will be the members of your community. A library, church, or community center would be a great place to speak. Be sure to ask permission and be prepared to explain what your speech will be about.

If your topic relates to both adults and kids in your community, ask your teacher if you may present your speech to your class. You may even get permission to speak to your entire school at an **assembly**.

Speech Tips

When you know the date and location of your speech, you can start spreading the word. Try making flyers and putting them up around your school or neighborhood. If00 your community has a website or social media page, ask a parent to post about your event. The more people who know about your speech, the more people your words can reach!

Research and Resources

To find out more about your topic, you will need to do some **research**, or careful study. The arguments in your speech should be supported by facts. For your antibullying speech, you may want to find facts about how bullying affects people. You may learn that kids who are bullied are more likely to do poorly in school. Also, bullied kids often end up bullying other kids later. You could look for examples of communities that have worked together to stop bullying.

You will likely use several **resources** during your research. These may include your school and local library, your teachers, and newspapers. The Internet is also a great place to find facts. However, remember that not all information on the Internet is true. Be sure that the websites you use are **credible**, or trustworthy. Websites run by museums, universities, and government agencies are good sources of credible, up-to-date information. To be sure your information is correct, try to find at least two credible sources that back up each fact you include.

Libraries are not only good places to find information. You can also use your time at the library to go over your sources and organize your speech.

Organize and Outline

When you feel you have done enough research and have the information you need, it is time to plan your speech. This process can be like writing an essay. The first step will be to sort your information into categories, or groups. One way to do this is with index cards. Think of each card as a separate section of your speech. On one card, you might write down all the information you found about what types of bullying happen in your community. On another card, you can write notes about how your community can come together to stop it.

Types of Bullying

- verbal bullying
- physical bullying
- online bullying

You can use your index cards when you deliver your speech. Still, you should try to memorize the order of your ideas before giving your speech.

It's a good idea to put specific numbers and facts that you find in your research on your index cards.

Once you have your facts sorted, try moving the cards around in different ways. Find the best way for the information to flow from one topic to the next.

Your speech should begin with an introduction. This is where you can introduce the topic to your audience and present your solution. The following sections of your speech will talk about the facts that support your solution. Your speech should then end with a conclusion. The conclusion will **summarize** what you have said, but state it in a new way.

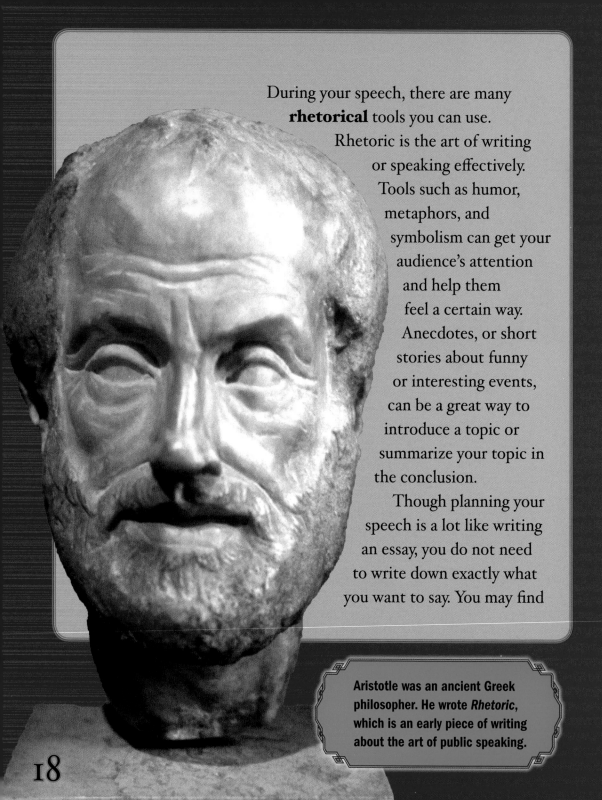

During your speech, there are many **rhetorical** tools you can use. Rhetoric is the art of writing or speaking effectively. Tools such as humor, metaphors, and symbolism can get your audience's attention and help them feel a certain way. Anecdotes, or short stories about funny or interesting events, can be a great way to introduce a topic or summarize your topic in the conclusion.

Though planning your speech is a lot like writing an essay, you do not need to write down exactly what you want to say. You may find

Aristotle was an ancient Greek philosopher. He wrote *Rhetoric*, which is an early piece of writing about the art of public speaking.

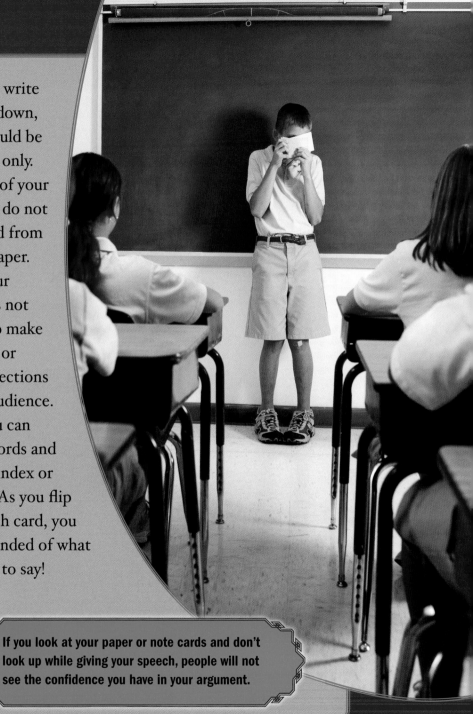

it helpful to write everything down, but this should be for practice only. On the day of your speech, you do not want to read from a piece of paper. Reading your speech does not allow you to make eye contact or create connections with your audience. Instead, you can write key words and phrases on index or note cards. As you flip through each card, you will be reminded of what you wanted to say!

If you look at your paper or note cards and don't look up while giving your speech, people will not see the confidence you have in your argument.

Get the Picture!

You may want to use a visual aid in your speech. This could be a graph, chart, photograph, or even a short video. Visuals, or things that people can see, are useful for getting across information that may be difficult or time-consuming to explain with words. For example, a graph can easily and quickly show how many people report being bullied or how many people say they have bullied others. Photos of kids who look sad because they have been bullied can create an emotional response in your audience. However you

You can use graphs to show trends. Trends are when something happens more or less often over time.

choose to use visuals, make sure that they present new information and do not just repeat what you have stated in your speech.

If you are giving your speech somewhere without access to electricity, you can use posters and an easel to present your visuals. If you do have access to electricity, though, consider using resources such as PowerPoint and Apple's Keynote to create and show visuals on a computer or tablet.

Speech Tips

If you would like to use visuals, keep this is mind when you are choosing a location to give your speech. Be sure you will have access to all the technology you will need, such as microphones, projectors, and computers or connections for your personal computer. If you would like to show a video, be sure you have a screen large enough for the audience to see it clearly.

Practice

You have probably heard the phrase "practice makes perfect." When it comes to giving a speech, that is the truth! Practicing your speech will let you hear how it sounds out loud. You can then change parts that do not make sense or flow well. Practicing can also help you feel more confident and less nervous when you are in front of a large audience!

Try giving your speech in front of a mirror. This may help you remember to look at your audience during your speech.

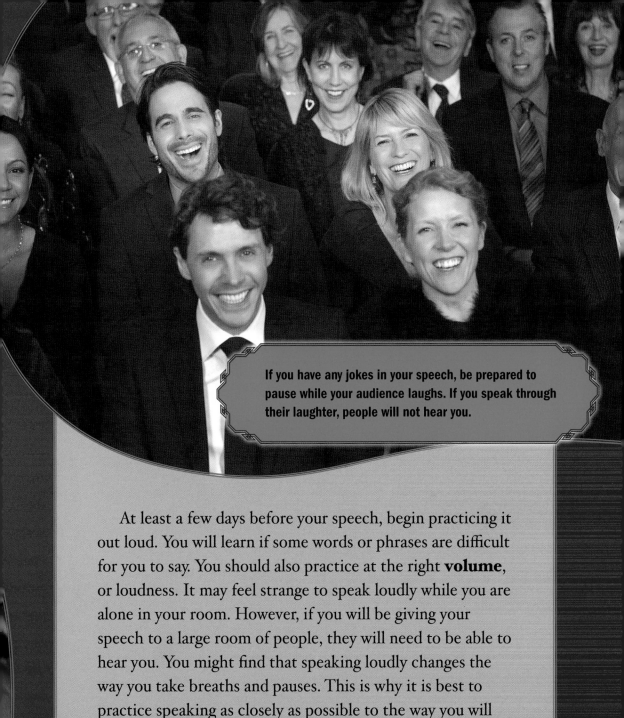

If you have any jokes in your speech, be prepared to pause while your audience laughs. If you speak through their laughter, people will not hear you.

At least a few days before your speech, begin practicing it out loud. You will learn if some words or phrases are difficult for you to say. You should also practice at the right **volume**, or loudness. It may feel strange to speak loudly while you are alone in your room. However, if you will be giving your speech to a large room of people, they will need to be able to hear you. You might find that speaking loudly changes the way you take breaths and pauses. This is why it is best to practice speaking as closely as possible to the way you will speak on the big day.

23

Once you feel comfortable with your speech, ask a few friends or family members to act as an audience and listen. Present your speech to them as you would on the big day, with pauses, gestures, and visuals. As you speak, watch to see if they are paying close attention and seem interested in your speech. When you are finished speaking, ask your audience for **feedback**, or comments and suggestions. Ask them to be honest so that you can use their feedback to improve. You may even ask them questions such as, "What was your favorite part?" or "Were there any parts that seemed confusing?" You can also try recording yourself on video as you practice your speech. You can watch the video after and look for anything that you would like to change.

You should also try timing your speech. This will give you an idea of how long you will speak on the big day. If your speech can be only a certain length of time, you will need to decide which parts to take out or shorten.

> If your audience just says, "It was great," ask them to tell you more! You want to know specifically what makes your speech good and how it can be improved.

The Big Day

The day of your speech has arrived! Many people feel nervous about speaking in front of others. If you do feel nervous, know that it is completely normal.

On the day of your speech, try to arrive at the location early. This will give you time to set up all the materials you need. You should check to be sure the microphones work and that all of your visuals are ready. Getting there early will also give you time to get comfortable in the room. You might find it helpful to stand on the stage and take a few deep breaths to relax.

This girl is going over her speech notes on a tablet. Be sure that your speech is fresh in your mind before you go on stage.

If you can, arrive early on the day of your speech. This way, you can get a feel for the stage and the size of the room.

As people begin to arrive, greet some of them and introduce yourself. You might ask people how they heard about your speech and if they are familiar with the issue. Getting to know a few audience members beforehand will help you feel more comfortable when it is time for your speech. Think of it as talking to a group of friends instead of a group of strangers.

When you begin your speech, introduce yourself to the audience. This will tell them who you are as well as give you a moment to get comfortable onstage.

When people get nervous, they often rush through their words and speak quickly. This makes it harder for an audience to follow the ideas being presented. As you speak, remember to take your time. If you lose your place, do not worry. Use your index cards to remind you of what you wanted to say. It is always better to take a moment and get back on track than to speak off topic.

If you would like to have your speech filmed, ask someone to do this for you ahead of time. With a parent's permission, you can put the video online and bring more attention to your cause. You can also email the video to people who were unable to come to see your speech.

You can ask your parents or a close friend to film your speech for you.

Speech Tips

Giving your speech may inspire you to start your own website about an issue. You can include a video of your speech, as well as the text of the speech for people to read. You can also include more information about the issue and a list of resources where people can find out more. Include links to other sites that you think are useful.

Learning and Growing

When your speech is over, take some time to think about how it went. Were you happy with your presentation? Were there things that you would like to work on for next time? Maybe you felt most comfortable telling funny anecdotes but felt like you did not make enough eye contact with the audience. Knowing your strengths will help you plan for your next speech. Knowing your weaknesses lets you know what you will need to work on!

If you feel passionate about your issue, consider getting involved with a local club or organization that supports the cause. You may even be asked to give another speech to a different group of people. Being able to speak comfortably and confidently in public is one of the most useful skills you can learn. Each time you speak in public, you are building even more confidence for the next time!

In many schools, a student will give a speech during a graduation ceremony. If you enjoyed giving your speech, make giving the graduation speech one of your future goals!

Glossary

argument (AR-gyoo-mint) A statement meant to persuade.

assembly (uh-SEM-blee) A gathering of people.

audience (AH-dee-ints) A group of people who watch, listen to, or read something.

awareness (uh-WER-nes) Knowledge of what is going on around you.

credible (KREH-duh-bel) Believable and trustworthy.

feedback (FEED-bak) Suggestions from people who have reviewed something.

motivate (MOH-tih-vayt) To give someone a reason to do something.

persuade (per-SWAYD) To argue for and get someone to do something.

research (rih-SERCH) Careful study.

resources (REE-sawrs-ez) Supplies, sources of energy, or useful things.

rhetorical (rih-TAWR-ih-kul) Having to do with the art of writing or speaking effectively.

summarize (SUH-muh-ryz) To make a short account of something that has been said or written.

volume (VOL-yum) Loudness.

Index

Websites

Due to the changing nature of Internet links, PowerKids Press has developed an online list of websites related to the subject of this book. This site is updated regularly. Please use this link to access the list: www.powerkidslinks.com/beacl/spee/